CW00786674

THE CAT'S PYJAMAS

THE CAT'S PYJAMAS

DAVID ROBILLIARD

THE BAD PRESS
MANCHESTER

First published in the United Kingdom in 1991 by The Bad Press.
9 Cranbourne Road, Chorlton, Manchester M21 2AP in an edition
limited to 1,000 copies.

Typeset printed and bound by Manchester Free Press, Paragon Mill, Jersey Street,
Manchester M4 6FP. Telephone 061-236 8822
Distributed in the U.K. by Turnaround distribution
Special thanks to Catherine Brown for her help in compiling David's work
Selection chosen by Robert Cochrane, Catherine Brown and Andrew Heard
Photograph on back cover by Dan Lepard
Designed by Robert Cochrane
ISBN 0 9517233 0 8

CONTENTS

31.3.84	1
THE REAL STAR	2
X-RAY VISION	3
THE HUMAN SPIRIT	4
ADONIS TIES THE KNOT	5
RUSHING TO FREEDOM	6
SMALL WORLD ISN'T IT	7
WHICH ISN'T VERY OFTEN	8
I WANT TO GO OUT TONIGHT	9
WHAT WILL YOUR NEXT MOVE BE?	10
AS PRETTY AS A PICTURE	11
NEW MAN ON THE MENU	12
FRUSTRATED BEAUTY	13
JIM DEAR	14
EXCITING NEW PLANS	15
EVERY DETAIL OF	16
A PARTY FOR TWO	17
CHOPPER SUCKER	18
EXCUSE ME	19
LONESOME MAGNETIC HARMONY	20
IRRITATION	21
FAME IS FLIES ROUND A FRESH TURD	22
CHILD OF LONELINESS	23
RELATIVITY DOESN'T HAVE TO BE A THEORY	24
WHY DON'T YOU DIAL ORGYOGRAM?	25
KHARMA	26
THE PHONE RINGS BUT YOU'RE ENGAGED	27
BEFORE YOUR DREAMS	28
AN EAGLE WITH MIGRAINE	29
FLYING YOUR SOUP	30

CONTENTS

PAGE

MORAL OF THE STORY	31
EVERYTHING SUBJECT TO AVAILABILITY	32
LET BULLIES SIT ON THEIR OWN DISGRACE	33
GIVING IT ALL YOU'VE GOT	34
HELP	35
THE DETERIORATIONS OF DIGNITY	36
NEXT	37
A FEW PECKS	38
AN ILL WIND	39
STAR	40
MACHO MORONIA	41
GIVING HEAD	42
LONG LIVE THE NEW MOON	43
CHERRIES IN CHOCOLATE	44
HERE THERE AND EVERYWHERE	45
YOUR BEAT IN ME	46
HANGOVER	47
I'M GOING HOME ALONE DARLING	48

BIOGRAPHY

David Robilliard was born in Guernsey, Channel Islands in 1952, and lived in London for the last 12 years of his life, until his death in November 1988. He was discovered in 1983 by the artists Gilbert & George, who have described him as "the new master of the modern person".

An artist as well as a writer, he has had one-man exhibitions of his paintings in Germany, Holland, Belgium, and the United States as well as in the U.K. Both his words and pictures are complimentary to one another, offering a candid, spirited and oblique look at life. Having never been to art school or had any formal training, his work retains a freshness and innocence that few others possess. Esoteric, humourous and ironic, his wit and satirical sense of fun dominated whatever he touched. 'The Cat's Pyjamas' is the fourth book of writing by David Robilliard, and contains some of his best work, never published anywhere before.

31.3.84

In braille
and foreign languages
make 'em laugh at bullies
not victims.
My hands and eyes and brain
connect
to give my trains of thought
to anyone interested
in words and pictures
and word pictures
my work is my life
I am its wife
no divorce
no separations

THE REAL STAR

The sun is high in the sky
and all the shady people on earth
are in and out of doors
out of order
but in the words of the sexists
the sun is a lady
and shines on all
a thought bubble coming from the sun
might be headed 'SYMBOLLOX' and reads
"Mother Earth, Father Sun —
stop mooning over nonsense
with your chameleonic languages
and barbaric behaviour —
we all know darned well
I'm just a mass of burning gas
and when that stops
your goose is cooked
end of your religion
end of your life
and don't forget
I don't actually need you
space travellers come back to earth
like shooting stars".

X—RAY VISION

Yesterday evening George said to me "would you like to see something nobody in the world's ever seen before?" I said "yes" and he cut a lime in half, holding a half in each hand and said "the inside of this lime, nobody has ever seen it before."

THE HUMAN SPIRIT

Strawberry fuckfart
cornucopia of water-based orgy butter
they pretend they are disgusted
they are really jealous
and they don't need to be,
anyone can join in
but no,
they're more interested
in making money out of war
and doing domestic chores
yum yum cream bun

ADONIS TIES THE KNOT

I can read your mind
it's written all over your face
'I'm an adonis and don't I know it'
fortunately the balance is put right for me
by the knowledge that you're a slag

RUSHING TO FREEDOM

Growling and howling
and losing control
oh the human race
don't make a soup kitchen
out of my soul
people scream and shout
and get locked out
of their homes
and these days
not even gnomes
have time for garden parties

SMALL WORLD ISN'T IT

We carved our name on a tree together
it got cut down and turned into a newspaper
announcing us getting spliced

WHICH ISN'T VERY OFTEN

You're so outrageous
I fall asleep every time I look
or think of you

I WANT TO GO OUT TONIGHT

Fully descriptive
and cryptic too
what else can you do
the tides stopped
flowing together
when I realised
you weren't going
to lend me any money

WHAT WILL YOUR NEXT MOVE BE?

27 years never having seen a porn film
27 years performing in them
during the next 27 years
you were concerned with growing up
being educated
finding a lover
working
paying the rent
in the second 27 years
you found yourself in porn films
'till in the end you could find no work
and during that time
you concerned yourself with a mortgage
hospitals
buying children's clothes
finding child-minders
a pension scheme

AS PRETTY AS A PICTURE

You used to want me
now you turn your back to me
I remember when
you couldn't take your eyes off me
our hearts beat faster
when we saw each other
the disaster was
nothing happened
now it's
nothing doing

NEW MAN ON THE MENU

Hung over and in love
and late for work
is no way
to start the day

FRUSTRATED BEAUTY

Holier than vow
several fortunes lost
trust in meat
diamonds
are a gargoyle's
best friend
you had a large slice
of the action
last night
and yet today
you're left
with just a big hole
in your life

JIM DEAR

Dear Jim,
if you can forgive me
then you're a better man than me
my tongue became my executioner
so why should you ever trust me again
but irrelevant of everything
I really do like you a lot
I remember the genuine affection
you gave me the next morning in your bed
PLEASE DON'T HATE ME.

EXCITING NEW PLANS

Don't
shriek
hysterically
at
me
I'm
as
empty
as
can
be

EVERY DETAIL OF

Your boring life
with all its
co-ordinated flashy living
is totally dull
as far as I'm concerned
the thought of you
is like dead ash
on my dinner
when I'm very hungry

A PARTY FOR TWO

The other evening I suddenly was coming toward the conclusion that the party this person intended, extended only as far as myself. I was surprised, not interested, and as it was my turn to talk I managed to get myself out of it without saying yes. It was not sympathy that was wanted, or even just sex, I could see a life-long relationship wanted. I'd like a party for two with....but the difference with me is I wouldn't dream of offering. I hope you're eating well darling.

CHOPPER SUCKER

Pluck a truck
and drive it right
up the highway
rock my trains out
pop my stains out
push my trolley
up the supermarket

EXCUSE ME

'You look lost'
'You look disgusting'
'Oh.'
As the person that said 'oh'
drifts off to another part of the bar
the other person thinks
'I don't mind all the people
whose eyes say
where can I find
where can I find
where can I find
but they're not for me.'
This was about all the people
standing round
except the ones
who had eyes
like a jackal on speed.
Then this person thought
'When will I find the person I need?'

LONESOME MAGNETIC HARMONY

My destiny
a bed-settee
help me
I don't want to drown
in a semi-stranger's
eiderdown
a comfort
for anyone else
but me
I'm new
I'm new
to this city
I'll always pay my share
I'm willing to try
a flat-share

IRRITATION

You thought 'Ah sod it, I'm going for breakfast and work half an hour later to make up the time.' On you went from the café, having blown your nose on a serviette (as your nose decided to go watery when you were in the café). Of course you forgot you had a hole in that jacket when you put your hankie in it, and it was travelling slowly, irritatingly down your leg. The next thing was, a policeman stopped you and forced you to fish it out of your tight trousers. Awkward and embarrassing. When you got to work, your boss was waiting for you with all the chairmen of the board. They were all red-faced and angry with you. Why should they think such a humble peasant as yourself can make their dream come true? But just you wait 'till the Gods go to war and the universe screams and time stops.

FAME IS FLIES ROUND A FRESH TURD

When I thought
I was in with a chance
I thought thank God
I'm not famous

CHILD OF LONELINESS

My perfect friend
wouldn't smoke
or stare
at every other person
my perfect friend
would be with me
in the end
would banish my loneliness
would keep me company
be such fun
in mind and body
do you mind
I haven't got anybody

RELATIVITY DOESN'T HAVE TO BE A THEORY

The people that cry on your behalf
could never be the shadow of what you want
let alone those that you would die for

WHY DON'T YOU DIAL ORGYOGRAM?

When your other half
goes off
with your bit of spare
prepare for
emotional flares
fashionable passion
with a melody
touch of melodrama
cleaning your teeth
standing in your pyjamas
and going to bed alone.

KHARMA

Oh I remember you
you're my wife
from a former life
and now you're
my husband

THE PHONE RINGS BUT YOU'RE ENGAGED

The world is full of so many things
disappointment
other people's romance
classic teasers
bereavement
fulfillment
choice
lack of choice
taste
lack of taste
relief
dignity
indignity
and on and on it goes
and the curtain never closes

BEFORE YOUR DREAMS

The language of bodies
gets you into my net, pet
and oh the scenes
in a thousand reams
out in the cold
without your jeans
can somebody show me
what all this means?

AN EAGLE WITH MIGRAINE

Before I was born
destiny said to me
I hope you've got
a head for heights
I said I'm not sure yet — why?
The reply was
you're going to be very tall
then I said I know
and I'm going to be a mountain climber
who climbs the tallest mountain
and then stays there as a hermit.
Destiny doesn't go in for cheek
and turned me into an eagle with migraine

FLYING YOUR SOUP

Waiter
there's soup on your fly
or are you just pleased to see me?

MORAL OF THE STORY

If everybody was a nudist
there'd be no pickpockets

EVERYTHING SUBJECT TO AVAILABILITY

Walking along the road
you can see so many things
birdshit on secondhand furniture
someone walking along with a white overall
covered in blood-
a butcher on a lunchbreak?
Which reminds me
walking and living through autumn
about the winter
and you and me
I want you to cover me

LET BULLIES SIT ON THEIR OWN DISGRACE

The guards in the palace
tried to play havoc with Alice
till they realised
she owned the place

GIVING IT ALL YOU'VE GOT

Some people
have got a lot of love to give
some people
have a lot of hate to live

HELP

Either the body's right
and the mind's wrong
or the mind's right
and the body's wrong

THE DETERIORATIONS OF DIGNITY

A tube ride to another boring days work
every single person in the carriage
has a watch on but me
I can't see the time on any of them
I hate early morning hurries
10 to 9
10 to grind
my mind wanders as we drive along
sitting sideways most of us
the beauty I can see
but not hold
is the same as fool's gold
a shared look goes deeper
than any clever magazine or book
meanwhile in the desert
they are groaning and dying
in their millions in the African planes

NEXT

Me and the other boys
discussed being stood up
as we approached dating age
not realising
it was the ego game
of the war of the sexes
not realising
that boys are supposed
to experience anger
not upset and hurt
but I believe
it happened to me
when I was 14
and you did it to me last night
and this afternoon
I feel like crying.
The 'phone is silent.

A FEW PECKS

Why don't you come back
for safe sex
you know
cuddles
and a few pecks

AN ILL WIND

A cloud over my head
and two pillows on my empty bed
how silently and effortlessly
your love flies
away from me

STAR

I wouldn't say you were downstage centre
but when you get in the middle of the stage
and start jumping up and down
the floorboards go tidal
and everyone goes down
and the unfortunate ones
go over the edge

MACHO MORONIA

It's not a game
it's just a global mentality that prevails
and makes everybody suffer
men in their minds
women and children
in their bodies
medals medals
shoot women and children first
medals medals
coat of arms
code of honour
Honourable discharge

GIVING HEAD

I think I'll get my head examined
but by who that is the thing

LONG LIVE THE NEW MOON

The knight in shining armour
now sits behind the wheel
of a well chromed car
but still life
is a series of phases
till it phases you out

CHERRIES IN CHOCOLATE

The hotline to my heart
has only one connection
— you
I'm here and you're there
I'm just up from my bed
where dreams of you
filled my head
there are millions
of gorgeous bodies
and brains
but unfortunately
and unavailably
only one you.
Still, what we do have together
is better than the aloneness
I had before.
Everything and everybody
in the world
could not begin to satisfy
some people's greed
but you have just
a healthy amount

HERE THERE AND EVERYWHERE

Tough luck
a chastity belt
and a padlock
a horse
and cart
and an aeroplane
have got you
foxed again

YOUR BEAT IN ME

Can you feel the beat
of my music inside you
so many words
have already been sung
so many beats are repeats
I want always to be original
I want to give sunshine
high energy
and fun fun fun
music for eagles
can you feel the beat
of my music inside you

HANGOVER

The lonely grapevine
grew in vain
but the battery grapevine
fed my greed last night
and my fucking head's
exploding now
5 to 6
and sex with myself as usual
the person I was thinking about
knew darned well...

I'M GOING HOME ALONE DARLING

I'm going home alone darling —
try that one for sighs